Interpretative Guide to Western-Northwest Weather Forecasts

by Marian Blue

Interpretative Guide
to Western-Northwest Weather Forecasts

Published by Sunbreak Press
P. O. Box 145
Clinton, WA 98236
www.sunbreakpress.com
an imprint of Blue & Ude Writers Services
www.blueudewritersservices.com

ISBN-13: 978-1-7321287-0-5

Manufactured in the United States of America
This book is printed on acid-free paper

First Edition 2018

Cover art painting by Dean Gibson (Title: Crowded Highway)

This book is a whimsical look at weather forecasting terms in the western part of the Northwest. Information, though not approved or condoned by any organization or individual, is presented as accurately as possible although exaggeration may exist. While every effort has been made to ensure the accuracy and legitimacy of references, referrals, and source information, the author is not responsible or liable for any misrepresented information by such sources. All opinions expressed are those of the author who believes Western-Northwest forecasters demonstrate inspirational fortitude in weathering the complications of predicting this region's weather.

For Wayne Ude
instigator of 24 years living in the Northwet

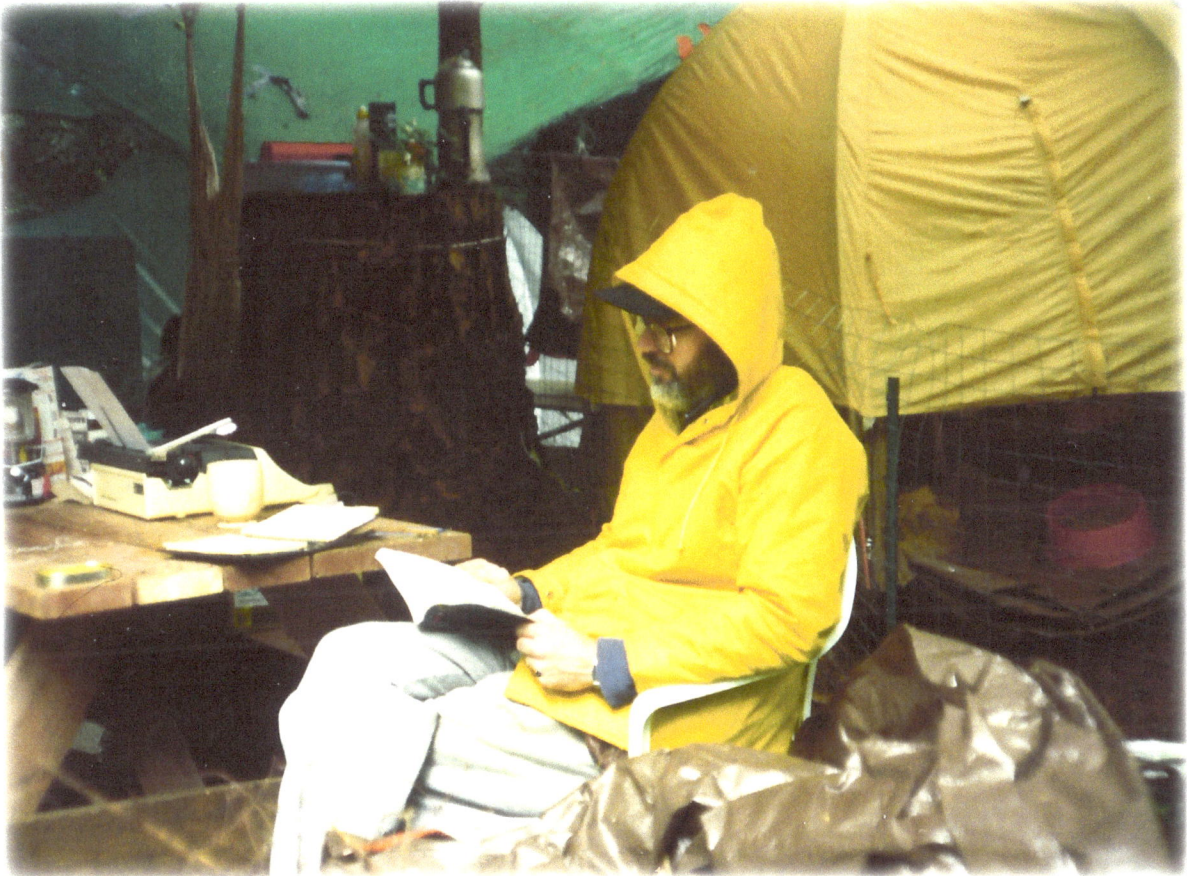

Summer camping on Whidbey Island, WA with Wayne Ude. A day with sunbreaks under the green tarp: no foul weather pants required. Foul weather gear, including rubber boots and tarps are standard summer camping equipment. If camping in winter, add an inflatable raft.

Photo by Marian Blue

Acknowledgments

Thank you to my readers, Sheryl Clough, Lynne Hann, Cherie Ude, and Wayne Ude who all helped me catch errors and illogical statements.

I also want to thank the many artists who contributed to this work:

Racheal J. Brager is a sixth generation Whidbey Islander. She loves long walks with dogs and capturing special moments through her camera lens while spending time with family and friends.

Dean Gibson pursues his art (oil on canvas) in the forest in Western Washington. The rainy climate inspires many of his paintings. His regional scenes with streetlights and reflected water are collected and displayed on both coasts. Dean's work ranges from figurative to abstract–often featuring bright, bold colors like those he encountered when he lived in India.

Lynne Hann, as a nature photographer, makes images of objects living in the outside world as well as those whose song has ended. Designs and patterns co-mingle in her favorite photographs while abstract lines, color, and dancing light gain her most constant attention. The Northwest is her favorite study hall. The variety of natural elements, geography, and conditions found scattered there hold her in a state of sustained passion. Lynne has had several public exhibits of her work and many of her images have appeared in magazines, books, calendars, and publications. For more, visit her Website at www.hannphoto.com.

Dan Lewis is a former long-time news reporter and presenter for KOMO-TV in Seattle, WA. For his work there, he received a dozen Emmy awards for Best Anchor in Seattle and also for reporting and writing. Now retired, he has become a photo buff and enjoys seeking out new locations to photograph. You can see many of those photos on Facebook at Dan Lewis News.

Danielle Pennington is a resident of Clinton, WA and loves photographing scenes of nature around Whidbey Island as a hobby. Taking photos of whales is a favorite.

Cherie Ude currently resides in Florida, pursuing natural images in the wetlands and on the shorelines. She also photographs special events, such as weddings, baby showers, family reunions, and other occasions. She has pursued photography throughout the U.S. and many parts of the world, including Europe, Canada, South America, Australia, and Antarctica where she worked for five years. She also lived on Whidbey Island for several years, capturing the many moods of the Western Northwest. Her images have appeared in many magazines, including cover art. See her images on Facebook at Cherie Ude Photography.

A very special thank you to our excellent government agencies who are generous with educational material, including permission to use certain graphics and illustrations in the following pages.
National Oceanic Atmospheric Association (NOAA)
The National Weather Service (NWS)
National Aeronautics and Space Administration (NASA)

Introduction

or

Wet Blanket Philosophy
For a Mildewed Culture

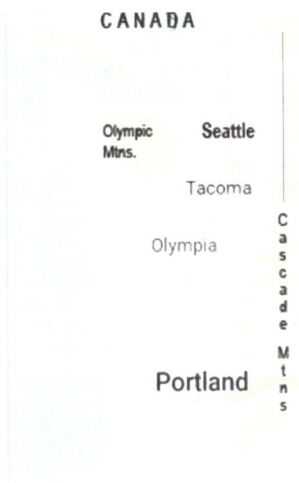

CANADA

Olympic   **Seattle**
Mtns.

Tacoma

Olympia

C
a
s
c
a
d
e

M
t
n
s

Portland

ONCE UPON A TIME, western-northwestern (otherwise known as simply the Northwest or Northwet) weather forecasters could say, "Rain followed by rain with heavy clouds and chill," day after day, October–May, without flinching once. In fact, gloomy forecasts were a part of creating the "It never stops raining in Seattle" mystique that kept incomers at bay, a goal of the time before the 1990s.

For instance, Oregon's campaign against incomers (especially from due south) included the Society for the Native Oregon Born (SNOB) that led the charge against invasions of new residents or tourists. Signs at state borders discouraged crossing the line. If you did cross the line AND you were from California, it was a good idea to replace car tags with those of a more benign state, such as Montana (a state that often claims to be part of the Northwest but that obviously lacks the required moisture to be part of the Northwet). SNOB is now related to designer beers.

Oregon Governor Tom McCall is (in)famous for his 1971 speech in which he said, "I urge them [visitors] to come and come many, many times to enjoy the beauty of Oregon. But I also ask them, for heaven's sake, don't move here to live." That was as friendly as it got and was more of a request for tourist dollars than the visitors themselves.

Meanwhile, to the north, Emmet Watson, a columnist for the *Post Intelligencer*, *Seattle Times* and other publications, created the Lesser Seattle movement. Aimed at incomers, his movement motto, "Keep the B*s*a*r*d* Out!" resulted in the acronym KBO. Watson referred to this group off and on from 1957–1997 in a backlash to the Seattle promotions started in the 1950s under the label The Greater Seattle. These were designed to encourage incomers.

About the 1990s, that "stay away philosophy" shifted. The major shaker for the change was capitalism. Big companies were going east to friendlier environments. In places such as Seattle and Portland, the desire to have city advantages (high-quality museums, high-quality public and private schools, symphonies, smooth roads, and, of course, a Washington State football team) required a population that could support those activities. Also, the established infrastructure needed maintenance. More people meant financial success in meeting all those needs through a well-watered economy, fertilized by thriving real estate sales, booming construction, and a strong tax base.

Publicists ramped up their praise for the advantages of living in the cool, beautiful, spacious environments that offered major water sports and nearby mountains with ski resorts in winter and wilderness hiking in summer. Touristy roads–such as The Mountain Loop, which is a conflated series of roads–were promoted. Both Seattle and Washington State went through a series of slogans to get away from descriptions such as "Rain Capital"; even "Emerald City" (that green came from rain, after all) was dumped for Seattle hip, such as Metronatural.

Magical moments abound when sunlight strikes sea blue among the isles of the Northwet.

Photo by Cherie Ude

At the same time, incomers stopped consistently hearing that the rainfall or dreary days would turn them suicidal. Rainfall was downplayed, not exaggerated, and pictures of sunny days on calm waters abounded: no moss, no fungi, no looming clouds. Forecasters wove the word *sun* into forecasts more often with terms that suggested that something other than clouds and rain were part of the predicted weather (such as partly cloudy, which suggests that something other than cloudy could be sun).

Today, incomers will hear nary a word about stormy moods. Locals probably won't even recommend reading *Sometimes a Great Notion* (Ken Kesey) or studying up on SAD (Seasonal Affective Disorder), which tends to be characterized by depression, exhaustion, and lack of interest in both people and regular activities such as caring about how many people move into the area.

However, the observant incomer may notice that sometimes around mid-*water year* (see *Year*), natives (and long-term residents of the Northwet) may become excessively ebullient when a February daffodil's spiky green is spotted. A mild hysteria rises with the cry of "Maybe *Spring* Will be Early." (Note that "spring" itself is not a reality in the Northwet – see *Seasons*).

Sadly (not related to SAD), many people who make the plunge and move to the Northwet because it's lushly green and gorgeous and because forecasters say the word *sun* often, swim to safety in one–two years and land in places such as Arizona. This keeps the real estate market active and, perhaps, helps fuel the reluctance of locals to say, "You're moving here? *REALLY*? Have you ever spent a year here?" After all, locals suspect the incomers won't stay long, and that satisfies the urge to keep the Northwet a private paradise while also keeping the economy active.

Consequently, saying "sun" often is part of the Western-Northwestern culture now. Examples include "Possible sunbreaks," "Lingering showers could let us see sunlight," and "Mostly cloudy with possible sun during the day." Any of these, of course, could mean that rain will fall profusely all day, so if you're a tourist or incomer, you may be confused if you hear what possibly

Northwet icon: Gray whale foraging in gray waters beneath a gray sky.

Photo by Marian Blue

sounds like a bright and cheery forecast only to find that you should have worn rubber boots, a rain coat, and a life preserver.

The definitions that follow may help you interpret forecasts and decide what you need to wear and what gear you should have when you visit or move here. The list is alphabetical with cross-references in italics when appropriate. This guide is **not** approved by any chamber of commerce or department of tourism or anyone worth noting, including weather forecasters.

§

Weather Forecasting Terms & Translations

Atmospheric River

An atmospheric river, usually called the *Pineapple Express* in the Northwet, builds up around Hawaii, gathering up the tropical moisture those folks don't want and then transporting it northeast to dump endless rain (or snow) on the west coast (the gift of the tropics). This hitch along the "global conveyor belt," which is referred to by NOAA as "a constantly moving system of deep-ocean circulation driven by temperature and salinity," is part of what creates Western-Northwest rainforests. Further study of wind and ocean currents will help you understand your need for rain gear in the Northwet. In summary, if you hear *Pineapple Express,* don't expect an exotic beverage; instead, blow up the dinghy and batten down the hatches. A grass skirt is permissible, but keep in mind it will probably start growing.

When day-to-day, noon-time gloom prowls the forest and surfs the waves, the sky channels a river, long and wide and here to stay.

Photo by Lynne Hann

Averages

Look up *climate* data for the Northwet–or anywhere–and the first concept that will pop up is *Averages.*

One needs to understand how the concept of averages is developed. Take all numerical figures over a decade, add them up, divide by ten and proclaim the result as an average. For instance, the average high temperature in Las Vegas is 80 degrees, according to the U.S. Climate Data Web page. Tell that to the hiker in July who is enduring 110 degrees for the afternoon. In another comparison, if I take all my weight averages each year since birth, add them up, and divide by my age, I can quit dieting.

In other words, averages ignore reality for mathematical simplicity. According to such mathematical magic, Seattle doesn't even make the top ten of the rainiest cities in the U.S. Almost the entire country east of the Mississippi gets more rainfall, on average, annually than Seattle.

Question: "So why does Seattle have the reputation of the place where it's always raining?"
Answer: "Because it's **always** raining."

Although the annual rainfall of approximately 38 inches in Seattle is about 10 inches less than in New York City's Central Park, Seattle receives that rain in a steady accumulation that adds up over months. Rain falls all the time (sometimes it isn't even "measurable," but you know you've been wet all day—see *rain* below for various names of rain-that-is-not-rain). On days when it isn't raining, the day is likely so dark that you have your house lights on all day and look out into heavy clouds or looming dark. You can enjoy high humidity (as in mildewed books) for 9–10 months a year; fog itself can leave you looking/feeling drenched.

However, in New York City, a downpour may drop an entire month's quota of rain in one day and then bring out the sun. Miami, which tops out with an average rainfall of about 62 inches, has fewer rainy days than the Northwet and, even on rainy days, tends to be warm with some sunshine. In other words, although New York City and Miami dump huge amounts of rain and then bring out a cheery day of sun to apologize, Seattle sulks and drizzles and weeps all the time. Think *kvetch.*

So read the averages and think, "That isn't so bad," but pack rubber boots and a raincoat with a hood—maybe a dinghy. Plan on buying a dehumidifier for your books.

Perhaps you'll feel drier knowing that the average yearly rain adds up to less than that falling yearly in New York City.

BURN BAN

Not truly a weather condition but related to weather in two ways.

First, a burn ban may be put into effect because of an *inversion (*see below), which usually happens in winter and results in stagnant air at head level and slightly higher and no rain to wash the air. The stagnant air is usually hazy and cold (fog, smog, pollution, and smoke) where people live, but higher elevations are warmer. In other words, if you want clear, warmer weather, go climb a mountain.

Second, a burn ban may follow a *drought* (see *drought/wet drought* below). The term suggests deserts, dust bowls, and dehydration. However, in the Northwet, any July week without rain represents a *drought*. Burn bans come in stages: 1, 2, and 3. Stage 1 relates mostly to outdoor burning and uncertified wood stoves and fireplaces. Stage 2 moves inside, banning fires in fireplaces and wood burning stoves unless that is your only source of heat (and it's cold enough that heat seems desirable, even to native Northwesterners). For Stage 3, don't burn anything, especially the rubber boots and raincoat even if you've been told that rain will never fall again.

CLIMATE

This refers to the weather conditions that dominate in a geographical location over a long period of time (see *averages*). Climate zones, or categories, are determined by combining details of geographic location, elevation, juxtaposition of large features (mountains or oceans, for instance), and how geography affects humidity, temperature, etc. Common climate zones are broad: polar,

A Cool, Temperate Maritime Climate makes farmers' soggy winter fields attractive vacation spots to snow goose visitors from frozen northern climates.

Photo by Lynne Hann

subpolar, boreal, cool temperate, warm temperate, subtropical, and tropical. This all seems very iffy in the sense that the number of climate zones range from 3 to 7, depending on which expert is counting. As a result, climate categories become hazy, rather like the Western-northwest weather.

In the "stay away" days, Western-northwesterners referred to their climate as Maritime Rainforest, and pictures featured the deep mosses that grew rampant in dark forests where families of Big Foot wandered. If stories were to be believed, house insulation expanded and smelled, turning to mold. Salamanders nestled in people's shoes.

Now, the same climate is often identified simply as Temperate, sounding rather like the perfect (maybe even tropical!) environment. Actually, if you add the "cool" and the "maritime," the description is fairly accurate (Cool, Temperate Maritime Climate) although NOT tropical. What this phrase translates to is that temperatures in lower elevations are mild, i.e., not as hot in summer as Phoenix and not as cold in winter as Duluth; the maritime, often omitted, means WET.

CLOUDS

The terminology for cloud conditions is extensive. Of course, clouds cheerfully wander the globe, inspiring painters and photographers. The terminology in the Northwet varies from other locations depending on which forecaster is feeling creative on any particular day. Northwet clouds are always lurking somewhere nearby (Wordsworth's Lonely Cloud is not here), so their combinations and activities provide diverse results. Cloud terms you'll hear in the forecast are, therefore, numerous. The following are some of the common terms in the Northwet with the most likely definitions any one forecaster may be using although those definitions, like clouds, may wander a bit.

BROKEN CLOUDS

This could indicate a *sunbreak* or mostly cloudy. Maybe *Light Spots in the Overcast (see below)*. The important message is that the **clouds are not really broken!** There will still be moisture in them, and it most likely will fall on you. Don't be fooled. Think of them as "leaky faucet."

CLOUDY

The clock may indicate that the sun has risen and is making progress toward the western horizon. Nonetheless, you have no physical proof. Dark. Gloomy. Use your car headlights and wear a headlamp. Make sure your cell phone is charged in case you get lost. You'll think it's just past twilight or maybe pre-dawn. At least lights will be on wherever people have installed those that come on automatically when it's dark.   Background cloud/fog/heavy mist photo by Cherie Ude

These Northwet clouds aren't the white, billowy, high-flying objects that look like ducks and dragons to those in Colorado lying on dry grass and looking up with undampened imagination. These are black, solid, even *mammatus* clouds (see cloud types); do not lie down with your mouth open.

When the weather forecasters deign to say "Cloudy" and never even mention *sunbreaks (*see *Sun)*, wear rubber boots and a rain coat (with a hood), and carry a life preserver because if it isn't raining yet, it will be. Your rain coat, or foul weather gear, should have reflective tape. Floods likely.

Light spots in the Overcast

"Overcast" means horizon-to-horizon clouds, or cloudy. Don't confuse "light spots" with indications of sunlight; the forecaster may be light-headed or spaceships may be in the vicinity. If it's kind of bright but gray, this could be *filtered sun* (see *Sun* below). Occasionally the gloom could lessen so significantly that you believe the overcast could dissipate. Don't cling to that thought, and don't go out on a search for the light spots (remember snipe hunts?). Keep the headlamp handy with, of course, all your rain gear.

Mostly Cloudy

Like *cloudy* but the headlamp may not be needed until after 3:00 p.m. The clouds are off the ground, probably over your head, especially if you're short (on the other hand, if you're short, always carry a life preserver). At times, you may think the day has suddenly lightened. This is temporary and is probably

Notice the life jacket warning on the pole under overcast or maybe cloudy or maybe filtered sun sky. Most people assume the sign is directly related to boating or maybe planned swimming. Keep in mind that both boating and swimming in the Northwet can come upon you unexpectedly. Be prepared! (Don't worry about the gulls; they are able to safely ignore the sign.)

Photo by Marian Blue

just a reflection of headlights going by. Don't lose the rubber boots and rain coat. In part, the term "mostly cloudy" is a relief from "cloudy" as it gives hope that somewhere you may find a place that isn't cloudy, so forecasters can boost morale through implication.

PARTLY CLOUDY

This is exactly the same as *partly sunny*, but it allows for variation in the forecast, and it hints at "mostly sunny." For public morale, including the word or suggestion of *sun* whenever possible is important. Besides, after several days of *cloudy* and *mostly cloudy,* people need encouragement to keep getting out of bed: *partly cloudy* is a psychological ploy forecasters use that suggests a progression, an improvement: cloudy to mostly cloudy to partly cloudy... Sun? Maybe. Don't worry about sunglasses and don't forget standard foul weather gear.

CLOUD TYPES

The Northwet has all the traditional clouds found wandering the planet plus an abundant selection of those uncommon elsewhere. Recognizing a few that are Northwet significant will explain native behavior under different conditions.

FOG

Although many people think *fog* is a separate species, neither cloud nor sun, it's a cloud, a very low and dense cloud, that has its own unique features and categories. The term fog sounds different from "cloudy," so the term adds variety to the forecast. See *Fog* below.

LENTICULAR CLOUDS (OR CAP CLOUDS)

If these layered beauties, built like flying saucers, hover over a mountain, two things are likely.

1) Most of the population will be outside taking pictures, many of which will show up as promotions on calendars, greeting cards, and brochures, all of which will be encouraging you to drop everything and come to this magical land of big blue sky and vast dry landscapes. However, that's Montana, not the Northwet.

2) The day is either *partly cloudy* or *partly sunny;* it could conceivably even be *mostly sunny* or *sunny!* Otherwise, if dense clouds loomed, no one could see the *lenticular clouds.* These lens-shaped clouds form when air cools as it moves up over the mountain, so the moisture condenses to form clouds on the summit. This condition frequently includes *irisation* (see below under *rainbow*), which means even more people will be taking pictures. The entire effect is pretty, but moving air can indicate weather ahead. Carry your rain coat and wear your rubber boots. Rain sleeves for your camera are a good idea.

Mt. Adams, capped lenticularly under an otherwise cloudless sky. Have rain gear in your camera bag.

Photo by Lynne Hann

MAMMATUS (from udder or breast) (Picture on page 20)

Heavy particles of moisture (frozen or not) cause clouds to droop, creating dark pouches beneath a cloud base. Often connected to thunderstorms (see *Squall* under rain), but thunderstorms aren't common in the Northwet. Both beautiful and surreal, as well as ominous, these Mamma or mammatocumulus creations can mean sudden downpours. Of course, you're thinking rain gear. Maybe life raft. Why are you outside?

THE BIG DARK

(coined by a creative forecaster on the Weather Channel 2017)

Should you be at a loss to describe the endless river of rain flowing across the Northwet, this term covers it well. The Big Dark that inspired this term referred to a continuous cloud line 5,000 miles long that knocked at least one forecaster into incredulity; consequently, the usual terms

The Big Dark: A Pineapple Express rides the jet stream into the Salish Sea.

Photo by Marian Blue

of *Pineapple Express* and *atmospheric river* were abandoned for a more descriptive term for the result, both in terms of weather and people's moods.

CONVERGENCE ZONE
(sometimes called the Puget Sound Convergence Zone or PSCZ)

Many people think this is a fixed location, like the *rain shadow*. However, the *rain shadow* is created by the Olympic Mountains, which don't move often although they sometimes shake. Being in the shadow means less rain; that shifts a bit, but with less regularity than the convergence zone (see *rain shadow*).

The mountains are connected to the convergence zone in that they cause winds coming from across the Pacific to split. These winds then collide like Sumo wrestlers on the other side of the mountains and become cranky, stirring up currents of air that rise, take on more moisture than they can handle and then dump moisture in that particular spot. In this zone, one can be in a deluge, while 10 miles north or south may even be *partly sunny*. This

Mammatus Clouds droop ominously; savvy folks are donning rain gear. The photographer survived.

Photo by Dan Lewis (with iPhone)

unfair distribution of rain can create resentment. Winds often converge, for instance, over Everett/ South Whidbey Island. If this has been going on for over 3 days, you may want to visit elsewhere.

Where this upper atmosphere collision will occur depends on many factors, including where the winds first split, how much moisture they carry, how fast they're going, and temperature in the various locations where the winds have been gadding about. Most people are convinced that wherever they live is where the convergence zone hits. People who live on South Whidbey Island **know** that Everett is the most common area for the convergence zone, give or take 28 miles to the south or north. If the winds are coming at the mountains from the northwest, the convergence zone can slide as far south as Tacoma, 60 miles from Everett; at other times, if the wind comes from a more southerly location, the PSCZ may glide north to Bellingham, which is 60 miles to the north of Everett. Just know that somewhere the *convergence zone*, rather like the Bermuda Triangle, is lurking. Usually, wherever the heaviest rain is falling will be identified by the forecaster as the convergence zone. If wind is blowing and clouds are looming, you can be 99% certain that you will get wet no matter where you are. Carry rain gear and maybe a compass and flashlight.

Sooner or later, the winds will rejoin and a tempest will ensue.

COOLING TREND

Probably indicates that a *Maritime Air Mass* is moving in. If you hear this when it's over 70 degrees and you see some sun, take sunscreen and your raincoat and your boots. When the cooler air arrives, the warmer air will have to shed some excess moisture somewhere rather like a Labrador coming out of the surf and heading for you. You have a 90% chance of getting wet.

DROUGHT

Imagine that through some fluke, no rain has fallen in a week (think August). Cities start to ration water. Counties pass *burn bans*. Foolish people fold up their raincoats and store them with their rubber boots in a trunk; umbrellas vanish (actually, that's always true–for more on umbrellas, see *Weather Gear* below). Sometimes, dry days can march along for weeks during July or August. The climax of this dry spell has a 75% chance of ending with a tempest that rivals Poseidon's temper tantrums, one of which may have inspired King Lear's quote:

> Blow, winds, and crack your cheeks! rage! blow!
> You cataracts and hurricanoes, spout
> Till you have drench'd our steeples, drown'd the cocks!

If you took advantage of a drought to store your raincoat, you won't stand a chance.

Most people in the world would consider a Western-northwest drought a pause in the weather; Californians would rejoice to have this kind of drought. People in Phoenix would consider themselves half-drowned in this kind of drought.

This particular casual use of the word *drought* is not to be confused with *wet drought* (see below).

WET DROUGHT

Although ironically more serious than a Northwet dry drought, a wet drought is invisible to the soggy eye peering out from under a waterproof hood on a typical Northwet day. Rather, this drought occurs because warmer temperatures (related to climate change these days) mean that rain, not snow, is falling in the mountains. Since much of the water supply in the dry season (see *drought*) depends on snow pack, the Northwet is, indeed, suffering from drought.

This will be the case even if you are swimming to

A typical Wet Drought dumps rain instead of snow in the mountains, which makes rivers flood in winter and then run low when water is needed in August.

Painting by Dean Gibson

work. Carry your raincoat and have rubber boots handy.

In summary, you have a 95% chance of getting damp in any *droughts* in the Maritime Temperate Climate although in July and August you also have a chance of getting sunburned. Carry water and sun screen in your rubber boots.

DRYING TREND

This is a term generally used to buoy spirits (like the suggested movement from *cloudy* to *partly cloudy*). The implication is that *drizzle* and *showers* (see under *Rain)* will continue over a long period of time, not that you can expect to have a desert gradually appear. If it rained an inch the day before, you can expect maybe only .875 of an inch on this new day. The term is relative to the answers to questions such as how wet has it been? how wet will it be? how long will the difference exist? Until you know the answers to those questions, wear a raincoat and boots and stay optimistic. You have a 100% chance of seeing August within 11 months.

EL NIÑO & LA NIÑA

Technically, El Niño is characterized by unusually warm ocean temperatures in the Equatorial Pacific; his sister, La Niña, is characterized by unusually cold ocean temperatures in the Equatorial Pacific. Both are, of course, related to the *marine* part of the Northwet climate. Also, neither presents anything you can point at and say, "Look, a Niño!"

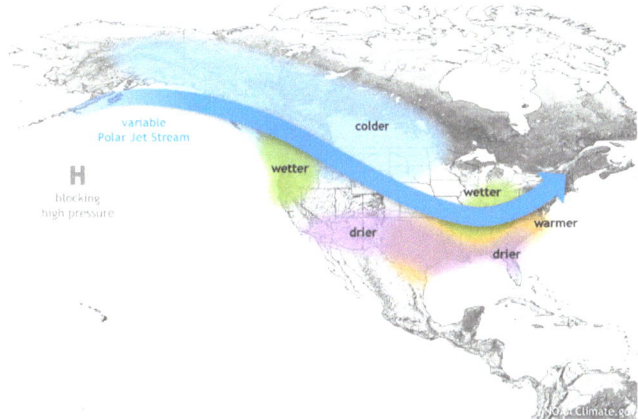

WINTER LA NIÑA PATTERN

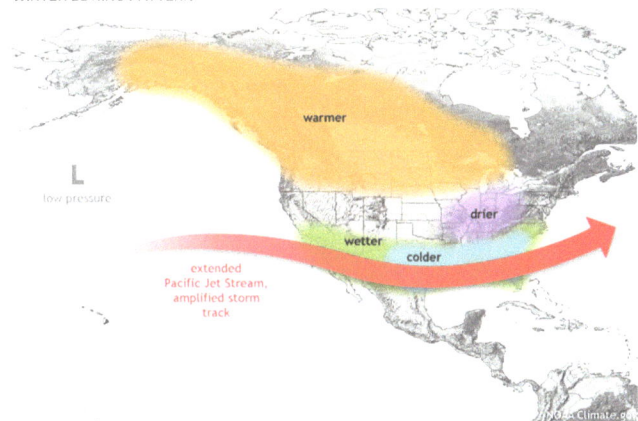

WINTER EL NIÑO PATTERN

Special thanks for Charts from NOAA's Climate.gov Website

Supposedly, La Niña can indicate that the Pacific Northwet winter will be wetter and chillier than usual. In contrast, El Niño years are supposed to offer the Northwet warmer temperatures and less rain.

These are both "tendencies" (see *Averages* to understand the ambiguity of the word "tendency"), but the differences are sufficient to keep happy those who measure rain in millimeters. For residents, the difference is negligible–keep in mind that the likelihood is that you'll be wet: keep your rubber boots, rain gear, and life jacket handy regardless of which child is calling. Also, keep in mind that children everywhere have a mischievous side.

What is significant for these kids is that the *jet stream* tends to hang around over or north of the Northwet when La Niña is around. This tends to bring many storms into the Puget Sound lap (see *Pineapple Express* under rain), so maybe keeping thermal underwear and a boat handy is a good idea, too. When El Niño comes to call, the jet stream tends to take storms more to the south. Mostly. Unless they are somehow magically attracted to the Northwet. If the forecaster mentions La Niña in particular, you may want to plan a winter vacation ... or dig a moat.

FOG

Fog and bodies of water go together, and, as with fog anywhere, can be confused with *mist* (see rain/mist). However, *mist* tends to be less dense and to feel damper; otherwise, mist, fog, and murk are interchangeable words. *Fog* is caused when lots of water vapor is suspended in the air, making visibility hazy to impossible. It's a little like swimming underwater except that swim goggles don't improve visibility. Fog can range from romantic and mystical (think Bogart and Rains strolling away to form their friendship) to plane-grounding, dense, blinding clouds, which also has a chance of being romantic but is more likely to be like Carpenter's *The Fog*.

ADVECTION FOG

Very common in the Northwet. This occurs typically when sea fog snakes inland over the cool land. Movement tends to be lateral and can be so thick that one can't see the road immediately in front of one's car. Headlights tend to blank out against the moisture in the air, so fog lights on cars are common. Staying snuggled inside is an excellent method of avoiding getting lost or run over by a driver who thinks maybe he can see where he's going because he has fog lights. This fog, rather like Sandberg's fog on cat feet, can come and go suddenly on land and on water. The good thing about fog is that you tend to get wet from the air itself: no rain (usually)! Of course, an umbrella is useless since this is more like being in a chilly sauna than rain.

Fog graces each month of the year in the Northwet, so rain gear may not be wanted, especially at the beach. But don't forget the emergency whistle, especially for children running into magical, misty spaces (unless it's La Niña or El Niño–they'll be just fine).

Photo by Lynne Hann

Rain gear that covers head to toe is good. And rubber boots (you may not be able to see puddles to avoid them). Again, staying inside is an excellent idea.

Freezing fog

Occurring when the fog moves in where air temperatures are below freezing, this treacherous condition can build up ice on tree branches and power lines, breaking them from the weight and turning the outdoors into a "Heavy, heavy hangs over thy poor head" game with nothing to win but the bonk. A hard hat is a good addition to your weather gear.

Freezing fog sculptures grow because water droplets are akin to the well-behaved child who joins forces with another child to become a large and destructive force; conditions change suddenly.

Expect ice to make surfaces, such as sidewalks, roads and bridges, into skating rinks; in addition, the fog often remains, making visibility moot, so you can't tell who has fallen in front of you.

Again, umbrellas are useless; the air is wet and everything else is slick. In fact, this is the time to be inside an unmovable object, like your house.

Freezing fog isn't as bad as *freezing rain,* but it's not user-friendly. Your raincoat will help, but few rubber boots have cleats to grip the ice. However, attachments with spikes

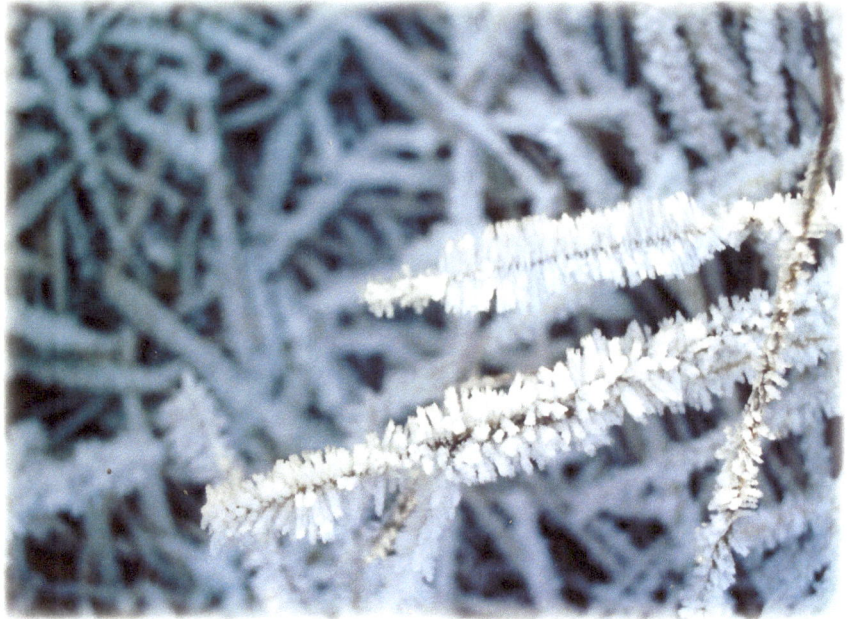

Freezing fog creates sculpture out of everything it touches. If the fog leaves and sunlight appears, the world is transformed into holiday brilliance.

Photo by Marian Blue

can be made a part of your Northwet weather survival kit. There is a reason these spikes are manufactured, and freezing fog and rain are part of that reason.

RADIATION FOG

This gloom is very common everywhere (involving the earth cooling the air) except, perhaps, in Phoenix. At least it isn't freezing, but it can still limit visibility to inches.

RIVER OF CLOUDS

One forecaster came up with this name to identify, apparently, the large fog banks (advection fog) that flow along the water, weaving between islands. Anything over 200' elevation usually remains in the clear even though endless fog horn moans rise like omens of doom from the solid white mass.

The primary thing to remember about fog is that it can happen anywhere, any time. Keep in mind that fog is made up of water particles. No rain falls, but you'll get wet. If you insist on venturing outside, you'll need good fog headlights and windshield wipers on your car. A fog horn can be useful especially if you venture outside on a bicycle (why would anyone do that?). Wear raingear with reflective tape and a headlamp. The best approach is to make popcorn and, snuggled in a fleece blankey, watch an old romantic movie while sitting in front of a wood stove.

A river of clouds flows silently along the myriad waterways of Puget Sound beneath shimmering peaks in clear skies.

Photo by Lynne Hann

FORECAST

Everyone is familiar with weather forecasts, but euphemisms often are used: Weather News, Weathercast, 5/7/10-Day Outlook, Right Now Weather, Likely Weather, and, of course, just Weather. Possibly, forecast sounds a little too definite.

Many words within forecasts are synonymous, too: interchangeable and abstract. Keep in mind that because many microclimates exist, caused by water, mountains, and elevation variety (not to mention pavement or forests), any forecast is to be forgiven if wrong. Most forecasters avoid the potential for being incorrect by using the percentage system to indicate the possibilities, likelihoods, chances of, and potential for weather (see *PoP* under *Rain*). Of course, weather is going to happen everywhere, but in the Northwet that weather is apt to be damp. Be prepared.

Another aspect to this weather business is that forecasters who simply offer "rain followed by rain" day after day lose followers; consequently, making forecasts interesting by varying the vocabulary is a good technique. Such variety gives the impression that the weather is constantly changing, so keeping tabs on it is a good idea although those changes may amount to no more than a 20-degree wind shift or 15 drops less rain per square foot.

In addition, the use of percentages (see *Rain* for more on percentages) is on the forecaster's side; keep in mind that the percentages aren't about the chances of rain or sun but rather the forecaster's confidence in her/his prediction. If Einstein had used forecasting terms, he might have said that there was an 88% chance that $E=MC^2$ within the scope of Earth's influence–for the next 7 days.

You can use your own significant method of foretelling the weather: if the forecaster in the studio is wearing a raincoat, get out of town.

FROST FLOWER

Frost flowers bloom only when the ground is saturated and the air temperatures drop to freezing (and below) without freezing the ground (freezing air temperatures, remember, don't necessarily mean everything on the ground is frozen). That is, the air temperature is below freezing but the ground hasn't yet been put through a "hard freeze." The reason the ground must not be frozen is that water needs to be flowing–wicked (capillary action)–upward into forest duff protrusions (such as broken alder limbs on the ground) where the moisture freezes when it's squeezed into the air. Water continues to wick up, pushing the ice layers outward. The layers freeze and expand, blooming frostily from the stick or other wicking item. Frost flowers can appear when no other frost is nearby although in open areas the ground or plants may be rimed. Rain and sun can ruin frost flowers, so if conditions are good, get out and look quickly. Forested areas are most likely to have good frost flowers. Wearing layers under your rain gear will help you feel warmer in the chilly and moist air.

Water wicked through decay to meet icy air where their union blooms in unlikely winter gardens.

Photo by Marian Blue

Frost gardens startle those walking by because little or no other frost is apparent, giving these gardens their own mystery.

Photos by Marian Blue

Ice transforms everything in the great Northwet.

GROUND CLUTTER

This sounds as though the forecaster is bemoaning the work of litterbugs in the area. In this case, the problem could be literally bugs if a swarm is large enough to show up on radar. This oddity further makes for uncertain forecasts and confused listeners to those forecasts. See more on this under *Rain, Radar*.

INVERSION

Normally, warmer air collects near the ground and the air cools as you go up in elevation. That's why it's usually cooler in the mountains.

In an inversion, high-pressure traps colder below. A high pressure system in summer usually just brings warmer temperatures. However, in winter the long nights allow heat to escape, rising away from the chilly people below. Then the warm air acts like a lid over the heavier, colder air. The lid also holds down all the pollution from cars, wood burning stoves, and those dreaded cow burps.

The stagnant, yucky air in lower areas results in *Burn Bans* to prevent worsening the air quality (not to be confused with burn bans during summer *droughts* when fire risk is present). An inversion often produces stable conditions but also a heavy cover of gloom, increasing SAD. Also, air quality warnings suggest not breathing, which can give the gloom more of a doom quality. Daylight lamps or trips up into the mountains to find sunshine are advised but take a raincoat because inversions can de-invert if a weather system happens to disturb the inversion lid. When a forecaster mentions an inversion, be prepared for murky but drier, maybe, air.

A hike to the top of Mt. Townsend at 6240' elevation reveals blue sky and sun above and trapped mucky air below: an inversion.

Photo by Marian Blue

JET STREAM

Of course, the jet stream belongs to everyone as do clouds. However, it likes to route itself directly over Western Washington in the winter, also like clouds. From the west, this powerful air current brings in the *Pineapple Express*, an air-traveling freight train loaded with rain (see *Pineapple Express/rain*), which it offloads smack dab over Puget Sound. See *The Big Dark* under *Clouds*. This is also related to *Atmospheric River*. All these terms mean that a massive water dump is present.

When the jet stream does a creative loop, flowing north up the coast then hooking to zip south over Puget Sound, colder air from the Frasier River in Alaska brings in the bounty of freezing rain and snow. Either way, the days are wet, maybe frozen. You have a 99% chance either way of suffering from extreme regret if you forgot your rubber boots.

If the jet stream is north of Puget Sound, not looping south until it barrels down on Idaho and Montana with Canadian gifts of snow and ice, the Northwet may be drier and warmer; this is an excellent time to ask for loans or to tell people about problems or to tell your significant other you are going to look for sweeter pastures because everyone is feeling beneficent. Do this quickly because the situation shifts rapidly, probably while you're sleeping and unaware. Meanwhile, locals start yelling drought and putting on sunscreen and sun glasses. Winter temperatures can rise to a balmy fifty-eight degrees.

Keeping an eye on the jet stream can't be done just by looking up, so forecasters' computer models are useful. Interestingly, Northwet forecasters rarely mention the jet stream; no one knows why, but it could be related to a desire to not disappoint people.

MARINE CLIMATE (also known as oceanic climate)

That's what you find along the Northwet coastal areas no matter how temperately the term is euphemized. Wet. Mossy. Rainforest. Big Foot. The term *marine climate*, of course, places all the blame on the ocean, but notice the difference between the Northwet and Southwest California and Baja deserts. Just having an ocean nearby doesn't cause saturated climates. Temperatures and mountains play into the mix, giving the forecasters a daily challenge except, of course, they **know** it will be wet for at least 9 months of the year. The challenge resides more within how to avoid telling people what the forecasters know but still recommend that people keep the rubber boots on.

Soaking days from wet air, even if rain isn't apparent, bejewel webs– and clothes.

Photo by Cherie Ude

The marine climate continually washes moisture over everything, making plant and moss growth prolific on the ground, on rocks, on tree trunks, and between your toes. One thinks elves must live here! Big Foot could be anywhere!

Rainforest photo by Marian Blue.
Moss photos by Cherie Ude

MARITIME AIR (MASS)

This is a large chunk of fairly uniform air, which is of course wet (hence the "maritime") in the winter and, sometimes, just cooler in July/August. This movement is called a "marine push" now and then; perhaps a "push" is less intimidating than a "mass." In the Northwet, a common winter Maritime air mass is polar and is related to a *marine climate*. Although likely (20%, perhaps, chance) drier than some systems that move into the area (such as the *Pineapple Express)*, these masses can produce long-lasting and widespread drizzle, fog, and cloudy conditions that make one wish to be somewhere else. Rain gear, head to foot, is best if this type of air mass comes along. Vacations to Phoenix are useful.

PETRICHOR

Petrichor refers to the aroma caused by various chemical reactions when rain falls after a dry spell.

Part of the earthy odor comes from plant oils, secreted during dry periods and released into the air when rain falls. Another contributor is geosmin, released from soil-dwelling bacteria. Humans are particularly sensitive to geosmin, which causes emotional reactions, many of which are related to memories of childhood when people looked forward to playing in mud puddles. This nostalgia aids survival in the Northwet.

Summer days hot enough to bring sunflowers to bloom are most likely to spread petrichor to our senses as the building clouds begin to unload their moisture. The aroma invigorates the spirit, giving people a sense that getting wet is okay.

Photo by Lynne Hann

Ozone adds to the overall effect when wind carries it down from the clouds. In Colorado, every afternoon thunderstorms produce this scent because the climate is dry (usually under 50% humidity contrasted to Seattle, which is usually over 70%). Residents of the Northwet are treated to this nostalgia-creating scent most often in July - September when the plants have had some dry weather, at least enough to accumulate oils. When someone waxes poetic about rain aroma, you're talking to a *pluviophile* (see below). Although it may have been dry, a whiff of petrichor should send you running for the foul weather gear not your childhood sweetheart.

PINEAPPLE EXPRESS

Drenching downpour coming!

The "pineapple" relates to the Hawaiian isles, which graciously donate the moisture. "Express" relates to the speed with which the moisture-laden air speeds toward the west coast. If the Northwet forecaster mentions this term, buy tickets to Phoenix or the Sahara if you have time. If you can't leave, make sure rain gear, including hip waders and life raft, are immediately to hand. See *Rain, Atmospheric River.*

The Big Dark seems endless because even though the storm is "express," thousands of miles of clouds take a while to pass. Think of one of those freight trains with a few hundred cars rattling your brain and patience, then add days to the experience.

NASA Satellite photo

Pineapple Express
Atmospheric River
The Big Dark
January Gloom & Doom

Understanding the weather behind these weather express trains may help ease fear and trembling that comes along with the forecaster's announcement that the train has left the tropics and is on the way.

Photo courtesy of NOAA

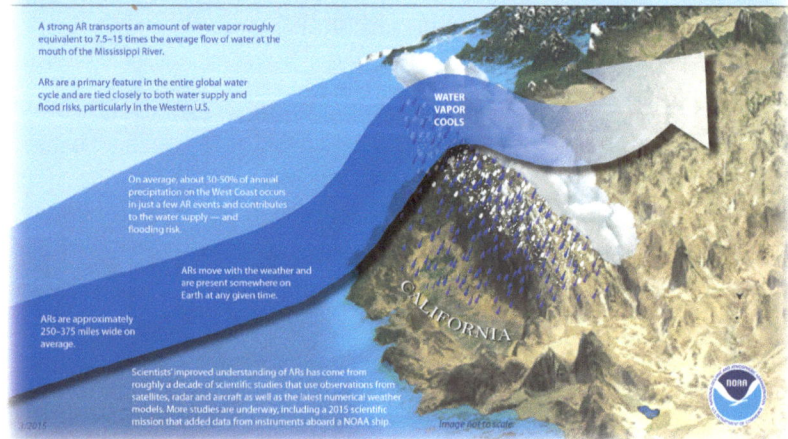

The science behind atmospheric rivers

An atmospheric river (AR) is a flowing column of condensed water vapor in the atmosphere responsible for producing significant levels of rain and snow, especially in the Western United States. When ARs move inland and sweep over the mountains, the water vapor rises and cools to create heavy precipitation. Though many ARs are weak systems that simply provide beneficial rain or snow, some of the larger, more powerful ARs can create extreme rainfall and floods capable of disrupting travel, inducing mudslides and causing catastrophic damage to life and property. Visit www.research.noaa.gov to learn more.

A strong AR transports an amount of water vapor roughly equivalent to 7.5–15 times the average flow of water at the mouth of the Mississippi River.

ARs are a primary feature in the entire global water cycle and are tied closely to both water supply and flood risks, particularly in the Western U.S.

On average, about 30-50% of annual precipitation on the West Coast occurs in just a few AR events and contributes to the water supply — and flooding risk.

ARs move with the weather and are present somewhere on Earth at any given time.

ARs are approximately 250-375 miles wide on average.

Scientists' improved understanding of ARs has come from roughly a decade of scientific studies that use observations from satellites, radar and aircraft as well as the latest numerical weather models. More studies are underway, including a 2015 scientific mission that added data from instruments aboard a NOAA ship.

WATER VAPOR COOLS

CALIFORNIA

Image not to scale

PLUVIOPHILE

A professed rain lover; a person who feels the rain in spirit and not just in the cold chill traversing the back of her neck. Pluviophiles often prowl the forests for fungus or moss, both of which also love rain. Forget about recommending foul weather gear and dry vacations in January to these individuals. One can only speculate that a certain number of years with moisture accumulating in the human system causes synapses to fire around any senses that should tell them that they're wearing moldy shoes. Pluviophiles are the founders of the myth that socks and sandals (See under *Weather Gear*) make sense in the Northwet.

Wet beauty graces the pluviophile's life in the Northwet.

Photo be Cherie Ude

When daffodils roll out sunshine promises in Skagit Valley farmers' fields, even sullen ombrophobes ignore the roiling clouds and attend the LaConnor Daffodil Festival (of course, they don't stay long, but pluviophiles stay the entire day–or longer).

Photo by Lynne Hann

POCKETS

This isn't just a place to carry coins and plastic rain shields. Again, because of the diversity in the Northwet landscape (sea level to high mountains, islands, and long channels from the ocean and down to Seattle), weather varies considerably. Temperatures shift around, just as wind does. Such variations can be just around the corner from each other. The term "pockets" makes such lurking weather surprises sound a little friendlier than warnings to beware of sudden chills and blasts of rain.

Forecasters often refer to *pockets* of weather (rain, snow, etc.) rather like various Mayors talk about road maintenance: the potholes don't go away and can't be predicted but no one is to blame. That's why you have your rain gear with you, right? You never know when you might fall into a Northwet Pocket or micro-climate. This may be why some rain gear advertises that it folds up so small that you can carry it in your pocket (does not include rubber boots).

PUDDLES

Speaking of falling into *pockets* and potholes, watch out for Northwet puddles. Yes, everyone gets puddles when it rains, even Phoenix. However, in the Northwet, as the rain continues, puddles shouldn't be underestimated. They could well be deeper than your rubber boots or waders. Indeed, entire cars can disappear in a puddle. Avoid them unless you're in a boat. Sometimes water erodes the ground and a puddle could be a sinkhole. This could be a direct route into Puget Sound. Rain gear won't help.

Following mariner traditions, sounding puddles may be the safest technique if you feel compelled to go near them.

Sketch by Dean Gibson

RADAR (acronym for Radio Direction and Ranging)

During WWII, military radar operators became aware of radar as a tool to detect precipitation, including snow and rain. This discovery wasn't a cause for joy because the weather "clutter" from storms obscured their targets, such as planes or boats. After the war, the Weather Bureau used radar to focus in on storms, and the technology became increasingly refined. Doppler radar came into use in the 1960s (utilizing the frequency changes, or Doppler effect, when radar waves bounce off anything in their path–related to the way a passing train will make a higher-pitched noise as it comes closer and a lower pitched noise while receding). By tracking storms over time, a forecaster can gauge how fast and how big storms are. Radar has become essential to forecasters who can "see" how storms are behaving while sitting, dry and warm, in front of their computers. However, radar readings can go awry with *ground clutter*.

<u>GROUND CLUTTER</u>

Flocks of birds and even massive groups of bugs can show up on radar, especially in the evening. This is because in the evening, as the atmosphere near the ground cools, the density of the air begins to increase (moisture increases until it becomes so heavy that it forms *dew*–see under *Rain)*. Having different density air at different heights causes the atmosphere to act like a lens. Since radar beams (waves) are just like light waves, they bend toward the ground in the evening, exposing the beam to much more of the dust, birds, and bugs near the ground. This results in false echoes. The image could be birds or bugs or, maybe, rain. Filters have been developed to help clear ground clutter from radar, but this continues to be a challenge at times, and forecasters, based on experience and the percentage system (PoP), have a 90% chance of being able to dismiss ground clutter from rain potential. This leaves a 10% chance that you may get wet unexpectedly. Add that to the 80% chance that, by living in the Northwet, you're going to get wet. That gives you a 170% need for rain gear. Radar doesn't change that.

RAIN

Sometimes forecasters become desperate for variation. One recently thought (apparently) that he was avoiding a gloomy forecast by predicting *showers* in the morning hours with the "likelihood of rain" in the afternoon with "increasingly wet" in the evening that would "decrease" overnight. In other words, "It's raining, Folks, and it's going to rain all day and all night!" At worst, his description confuses people, but they're probably happier than they would be with the idea of endless rain.

No wonder many forecasters' terms are interchangeable (rain likely, probability of rain, chance of rain, increasing showers, decreasing showers, scattered showers, occasional showers, etc.). If it weren't for the many synonyms of the word "probable" and the use of percentages, forecasters would be at a loss for how to convey hope. The synonymous terms allow people to hear, to interpret from their own perspective, and then to go on their way happy or depressed depending on their own natural inclinations.

The well-being of citizens and desire of forecasters to be liked has led, since the 1960s, to increasing use of percentages in forecasts. This has come about thanks to the work of the National

Weather Service along with many dedicated meteorologists. Perhaps percentages, along with synonyms, is a way to hedge their bets while remaining true to their meteorological calling. Pity the pre-technology forecasters who had to rely on leaves turning over or knee joints aching to predict storms. Technology, of course, hasn't improved forecast accuracy so much as given forecasters ways to improve their uncertainty presentation–even a turning leaf has a 50% chance of being right.

Beach Day in the Northwet, even in warmer weather, offers a 98% chance of being a day to watch the rain.

Photo by Lynne Hann

Keep in mind that PoP (probability of precipitation) is not the true chance of precipitation so much as the forecaster's conviction that rain will/won't occur. This is like saying, "I'm 35% certain Wonder Woman will become President of the United States." Even if this doesn't happen, you are still correct within the remaining 65% within which you were uncertain that she would take office.

The current PoP is based on "The Neural Network," which is an artificial network functioning in a nonlinear system that is, at best, confusing to even those using it, judging by the various discussions on the Web. If you're interested in expanding your confusion on the subject, you can see a video about the subject online under "Visualization of Neural Network Predictions for Weather Forecasting (VMV 2017)."

The PoP calculation method is also presented on a NOAA Web page, in part, as:

PoP = C × A where "C" = the confidence that precipitation will occur somewhere in the forecast area, and where "A" = the percent of the area that will receive measureable precipitation, if it occurs at all. So... in the case of the forecast above [shown on the Web page], *if the forecaster knows precipitation is sure to occur (confidence is 100%), he/she is expressing how much of the area will receive measurable rain. (PoP = "C" x "A" or "1" times ".4" which equals .4 or 40%.)*

In other words, rain may fall somewhere in the forecast area unless it doesn't.

As a clarification example of how percentages work in theory, here is a quote from the Vegas Online information about your percentages (chances) of winning on a slot machine:

… the chance of hitting, say a cherry on one line is 1/5. The chance of hitting a cherry on the second line is also 1/5. Therefore the chance of hitting five cherries in a row is 1/5 x 1/5 x 1/5 x 1/5 x 1/5, or 1/3125, or 0.032%. Your odds of winning are better than this, as you can hit five bells, five whistles or five of any other set of symbols, so on this machine your odds of any set of five are actually 5 x 0.032%, or 0.16%. So once in every 625 spins of this hypothetical machine, you'll hit your set of five identical symbols for the jackpot.

Still foggy? There is a 30% chance that studying quantum mechanics may help.

One simple explanation is that, ultimately, the house wins. Ultimately, it rains … somewhere … sooner or later … but maybe perhaps you have a chance it won't … so go ahead, go outside. Hedge your bets with (you've got it!) rain gear. Rain gear is a 100% good idea. Unless you're in Phoenix.

THU	FRI	SAT	SUN	MON	TUE	WED	THU	FRI
30%	30%	30%	30%	20%	20%	30%	30%	20%

Rain or not, the forecast above is correct because rain chances are only a possibility, in the forecaster's opinion, in any given area at any given time. In essence, if the forecaster avoids 0% uses, s/he is always right!

ACID RAIN

Even in the Northwet, the rain can't quite clean the atmosphere these days. This may be partly due to the failure of movements such as KBO and SNOB to curb the growing population if you're looking for someone to blame. However, much of the acid rain that occurs in the Northwet is related to volcanic activity rather than industrial waste. Wildfires, increasingly common, can also contribute. The good news is that the air is scrubbed on a regular basis (except for *inversions*), so if you don't mind the occasional ash fall, don't worry. Your rain gear probably won't melt.

CLOUDBURST

As with other places, cloudbursts (a lot of rain falling in a short period of time) can catch people off guard. However, this happens, perhaps, more often in the Northwet and the "short period of time" can be longer, say 24 hours–or days. The most rain to fall (described as "torrential") in a day in Seattle is over five inches. Related terms, not separately listed, are deluge, torrential, downpour, copious, relentless, scaturient … These terms are not often used by forecasters who tend to be optimistic unless actual flood warnings are extant.

Cloudbursts often are related to *squalls* along the coast, which, in turn, can be connected to lines of *thunderstorms* or *bands* of rain. If the forecaster predicts a "…wet day ahead …" you may want to make plans to find your snorkel and mask.

DEW

These lovely droplets bejewel plants and other objects when moist air is cooled at night so that moisture must be dropped (dewdrops). Although difficult to see in the rain, dew is abundant in (Northwet) *drought*s. This is related to *serein* although dew is not considered rain, mainly because the droplets don't coalesce in the air, so you can't see it before it accumulates on an object. Sometimes dewdrops and lingering raindrops look alike. Either way, should you walk through weedy or plant-bordered pathways, rubber boots will help keep you dry.

Dewdrops are nature's sequins for showiest wear.
Photo by Cherie Ude

FLURRIES

Because the phrase "snow flurries" is used frequently, many people believe that this term is all about snow, but those many are not familiar with the Northwet. Flurry, by definition, involves a sudden burst of activity, swirling around. In the plural, rain flurries, therefore, are sudden bursts of rain falling more or less vertically in various directions as it is being swirled by gusts. Because no one counts each flurry, the translation is more akin to "windy with light rain that is sometimes horizontal." Terms such as *scattered* or *isolated* may also apply. Head-to-foot rain gear is indicated for flurries in temperatures above freezing. If temperatures drop below freezing, see *freezing rain, mix,* or *graupel*. The implication is that a flurry is sort of fun and maybe even cute. That's true if you're wearing good rain gear and like being buffeted.

FREEZING RAIN

When *rain* falls onto a surface that has been laying around in subfreezing temperatures, the *rain* magically converts to ice. This is because water can avoid freezing in the air even if the air temperature is lower than 32 degrees. The ice not only accumulates, it can also be difficult to see on the road, steps, sidewalks. Staying home is an outstanding option; in fact, staying home from October to April is something to consider unless you're leaving on a plane, which will probably be grounded because of freezing rain. If you're going to muscle through the mess, in addition to the rain gear

Water moving through freezing air grows ice on anything it touches. This can morph ordinary objects such as trees into abstract works of art and streets into deadly skating rinks. If temperatures start dropping and the rain continues, expect schools to close and freeways to come to a stop.

Photo by Lynne Hann

(layered) to keep from getting soaked (since your temperature is probably above freezing), cleats or ice skates come in handy. If driving, prepare to appear somewhere online as a funny video of a car waltzing down the streets while the photographer giggles uncontrollably into the mike.

GRAUPEL

This term comes from the German and refers to "soft snow" or snow pellets. Although this can look like *hail*, it's softer since it's water frozen around a snowflake (doesn't necessarily need the wind that is associated with *hail*). The term isn't used often on weather forecasts, but many Northwet natives are connoisseurs of the different states of water and are apt to use this term when you may just see snow. Because it's soft, you can get wet, of course. And it's cold. Turtlenecks are snuggly if worn under, of course, rain gear. Turtlenecks without rain gear are just silly.

HAIL

This is rain that keeps getting tossed back up into cooler air, freezing a little harder and larger each time it's tossed. The strength of the wind correlates with how much getting hit by hail will hurt. The nice thing about hail is that it usually doesn't last long. The downside is that it usually turns into rain, which lasts … and lasts. Rain gear is, of course, essential both before and after the hail, but adding a helmet to the standard foul weather gear can be useful.

INCREASING RAIN IN THE P.M. (OR A.M.)

This suggests that the rain is going to be less in either the A.M. or the P.M., but this is ambiguous, depending on how much rain WAS falling and WILL fall–the only certainty is that rain will fall. Set aside the *PoP* and assume that this means, simply, *rain*, both before and after, in different amounts if measured in millimeters. Have rain gear with you in the A.M. and the P.M.

ISOLATED (OR BAND) OF
* Rain
* Showers
* Thunderstorms

Rain offshore marches by, a band in isolation.
Photo by Lynne Hann

Falling moisture in bands or isolation means that wherever you are, you're probably getting wet with the implication that somewhere else is dry, not necessarily in the Northwet. Like Phoenix.

The usual phrase "A *band* of showers across…" sounds rather festive, but if you go out to watch the band pass, wear rain gear as these bands lack a leader and can veer in your direction abruptly.

A new graphic has recently appeared on visual forecasts that represents "bands" of rain as brown lines, rather like rubber bands. When mixed in with the blue cold front lines and the red warm front lines and the blobs of pink, blue, yellow, green, and white, these look a little like earth worms seeking safety. Which is a good plan if you don't want to get wet.

Mix

This term is used in forecasts all the time, most often when temperatures are vacillating on either side of freezing. Wind, too, can play a role, tossing moisture in various liquid and solid states up and down. A rain mix usually involves snow (or sleet or some version of firmer rain) falling with the rain. Snow mix is not your romantic, drifting, ballet of snowflakes; this is stuff to bite your cheeks, make your eyes water, and soak your clothes. Layer your rain gear. Consider a helmet. This is a step away from both *freezing rain* and from *Graupel*.

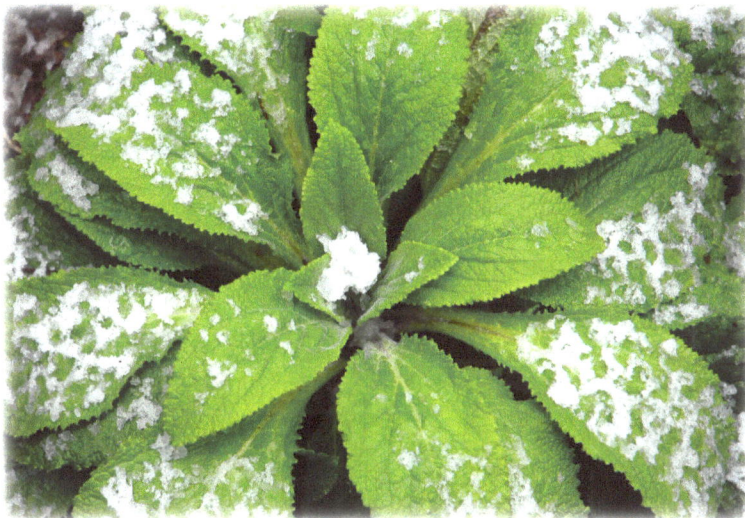

A little cold, a little graupel, a little rain, maybe a little snow: this mix can leave confusing deposits of wet and mushy white stuff. Sometimes a heavy snow is immediately followed by rain, which can convert the heavy snow into heavy loads that break tree limbs and collapse roofs. Sometimes the snow just melts quickly, causing floods. This is a Northwet mixed bag.

Photo by Marian Blue

Mist

Moisture particles cling to the air itself, not as fog because mist is less dense, allowing for better visibility. However, the droplets don't coalesce into a large enough size to fall. This is very common in the rainforest areas of the Northwet where and bryophytes, such as ferns, can live in high branches of trees, particularly big leaf maples and old Sitka spruce, and drink from the sky.

These plants include mosses and lichens. A rainforest is a wet jungle.

Even though rain isn't falling on a misty day, wearing rain gear will keep you from feeling sponge- or epiphyte-like.

Misty LaPush, WA. Not fog (too light). Not rain, not showers (no moisture falling). Just damp. Moist. Wet. LaPush isn't far from Forks, the setting for the vampire books/movies. Mist could evaporate. Or turn into rain. Or deepen into heavy fog. Or just stay gloomy all day. Don't carry rain gear ... wear it.

Photo by Marian Blue

SEREIN

Light *drizzle* (see *showers*) falling out of a clear sky, normally about twilight (cooling air can no longer hold onto its moisture). Serein is undeniable proof that clear weather requires at least a rain jacket. In effect, serein is so light that you have a 70% chance of not getting particularly wet. Probably.

SHEET

This word has two meanings. In the vernacular, "The rain is coming down in sheets" is akin to "It's raining cats and dogs out there." The saying about "cats and dogs" has many origin theories, but the earliest references (1600s) tend to offset the popular later story about heavy rains washing critters out of thatch roofs. For more details on the origin, check out the Library of Congress site on Everyday Mysteries. The reference itself is akin to *cloudburst* and related terms. Perhaps the sheet reference grew from the days when people used to hang laundry on the outside line.

Being out in cloudbursts, sheets, or torrents of rain can be disorienting, making walking and driving hazardous. Coffee, even famous Northwet coffee, won't help.

Painting by Dean Gibson

Technically (setting aside the cats and dogs), sheets of rain as a weather description can refer to a rainstorm in the distance as it passes, curtain-line, across the water. Distance shouldn't delude one into thinking that rain gear isn't necessary; sheets are related to *bands* and can suddenly swerve. So keep in mind while standing onshore and watching rainstorms move across the water that the peaceful, even romantic moment can change suddenly. You must always wear rain gear or be prepared to run really fast because getting hit by a wet sheet is startling.

SHOWERS

This is a brief and light rain in theory. The word brings to mind spring and lurking sun. Maybe Pat Boone and *April Love*. Drizzle, sprinkle, heavy mist, and light rain are all synonymous terms for shower. Also used are "Chance of showers," "Scattered showers," "Showers and *sunbreaks*," "Lingering Showers," and "Showers ending." "Passing showers" has been coming up more often.

Don't most showers pass? Well, maybe not in the Northwet. "Lingering showers" can go on for days, even after the sun comes out as trees slowly drip dry.

Expect to be wet. Wear a raincoat and carry rubber boots.

Sirimiri

Although a Spanish term, it fits the heavy *mist* that isn't quite rain and that sometimes is interspersed with foggy-like conditions. The British may refer to this as "dampish out," but in Northwet terms, it's just a "nice day."

Sleet

Go inside!

Not-quite-frozen rain (which would be *hail*). Sleet is complicated rain that starts out falling normally. Then it falls through a cold layer. At that point, a snowflake forms, melts partially in the next thin layer of warmer air, and then, encountering a layer of colder air, freezes before it hits the ground (unlike *freezing rain* which doesn't freeze until it impacts an object). This creates ice pellets, not as potentially large as *hail* nor as soft as *Graupel,* although the effect is still chilling and dampening. In addition, since it's not uncommon to have wind swirling through the situation, sleet feels like having sand thrown against your skin. Padding helps. Layer your rain gear. Wear a helmet. Better yet, as mentioned above, go inside!

Snow

Snow in the lower elevations of the Northwet tends to be heavy, moist, and short-lived. However, now and then the light, fluffy flakes do drift lazily down. People usually rush outside to enjoy the experience because rain will probably mush it up quickly. That's why snow (and hail, etc.) is listed under "rain." It's all water!

Because the snow is heavy, evergreen limbs bend then break, so if you're out enjoying the snow, try to stay away from big trees. Roofs also collapse, so maybe outside in an open field is

Lingering showers indicate a good day to wear a rain hood and rubber boots that are at least ankle-high.
Photo by Cherie Ude

Snow, the fluffy kind, tends to surprise everyone when it visits the Northwet.
Photo by Marian Blue

the safest location. Add a hard hat again to your foul weather gear.

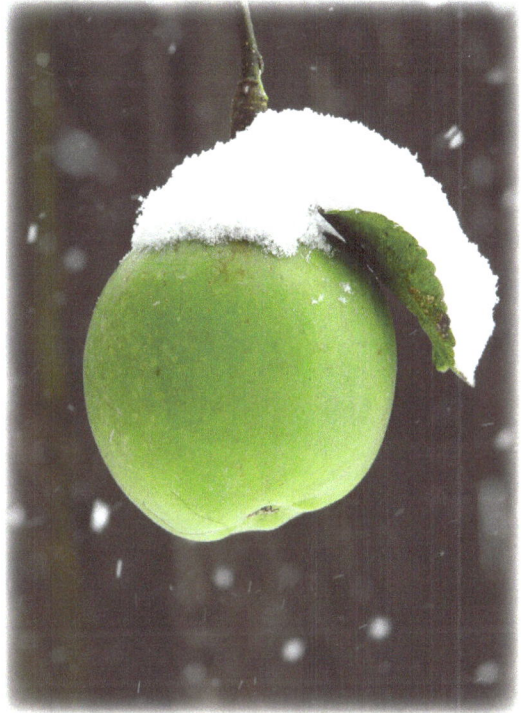

No one can resist genuine snow in the Northwet as it transforms the ordinary into the whimsical.
Photo by Cherie Ude.

SQUALL

Because thunderstorms are uncommon, this term isn't used by forecasters much, but periodically a line or *band* of thunderstorms marches along the waterways of Puget Sound. When this happens, the results get the attention of everyone with high winds, vivid lightning, and rolling thunder. May 4, 2017 brought such a vigorous storm. The National Weather Service recorded 2500 lightning strikes in Western Washington. This is the same year that was unusually warm and that also had set records for rainfall October-May at almost 46 inches.

During that May storm, the wind whipped along with enough force to break and knock over trees. Transformers exploded and power lines fell.

That's a squall.

Should the forecaster say squalls, expect lots of drama followed by many pictures of lightning strikes that occurred near the Seattle Space Needle. Neither a hard hat nor rain gear protects from lightning.

VIRGA

Virga isn't common in the Northwet because dry air needs to be present to evaporate water drops falling from a cloud **before** the droplets reach the ground (or water) below. However, virga is sometimes mentioned by forecasters in an offhand way, usually during a July *drought* as in "It's just virga." No one wants to be "just" anything, so virga tends to reside in Phoenix.

§

Ultimately, rain means only "wet" no matter what the falling moistrue is called. The speed, intensity, and consistency vary considerably from micro-climate to pocket, from convergence zone to rain shadow–hence the vast and creative vocabulary of rain words, especially in the Northwet–that and the forecasters seeking, as mentioned before, variety. Simply saying "rain" is known as stating the obvious. Like telling people to wear rain gear.

RAINBOW–SKY COLOR

A host of words goes with the concept of rainbows–light/color shows–in the Northwet. A complete and bright rainbow across the entire sky isn't that common because there's at least a 50% chance that it will be too cloudy along the projected rainbow route for sunlight to create the effect, but a host of similar light shows make up for the lack. Many of these are identical, including fogbows, crepuscular/anticrepuscular rays, glories, glorioles, halos, nimbi, sundogs (parhelia), sun spokes, irisation, and moonbows. All of these, and others, involve water particles (frozen or not)

Clouds and moisture combine to paint the days with color and promises of ever more beauty to come.

Photo by Cherie Ude

bending and playing with light waves, creating color. Although they show up all over the world, they live in the Northwet where the well-hydrated atmosphere and shy light love to play and experiment.

Rings around the sun usually occur when a fairly even layer of cirrostratus clouds coats the sky, bending light in a consistent pattern. Before the radar, satellites, and computers, light and clouds were read by people to predict weather. Percentages weren't used, so prediction came as a fact. A ring around the sun or the moon meant rain would soon arrive.

Photo by Cherie Ude

Light, clouds, water... the signature elements of the Northwet climate, are the artists of sky color and special effects, such as these crepuscular rays.

Photo by Marian Blue

Northwet sunsets, spectacular, frequently grace even dreary days.

Photo by Marian Blue

The sun silvers a slice of moon and simmers the Northwet sky with glowing embers.

Photo by Lynne Hann

RAIN SHADOW

Because the Olympic Mountains jut out of the Olympic Peninsula, some weather off the Pacific is redirected. Winds are forced to rise over the mountains (orographic lifting) or to go around them; the rising air cools, and moisture falls, so when the air reaches the other side, it's drier. The result is that one side of the mountain range is wetter (rain forest) and the other side is the banana belt (think of The Blue Hole of Sequim, which is highly promoted on the Internet).

By studying average rainfall in the area, the effect of the rain shadow becomes apparent. For instance, Sequim gets 16.5 inches of annual rainfall and Mt. Olympus gets 220 inches. In a direct line (crow flight), Sequim is 34 miles from Mt. Olympus. Not only are your feet drier in Sequim, but your head will experience more direct sun, kinder winters, and less need for rain gear (that's LESS need, not NO need) than almost anywhere else in the Northwet. In fact, The Blue Hole of Sequim is desert-like, and early farmers discovered that rain was insufficient for crops; irrigation was needed.

If moving to the maritime climate, check out where your ideal location falls on the 220 inches vs. 16 inches of rainfall scale (yes, people do live/swim in the rainforest).

On an even smaller scale, Whidbey Island offers a drastic change in precipitation, which can be seen in flora (cactus such as *Opuntia fragilis* in Coupeville and moss in Clinton, just 20 miles away) and fauna (lizards in Coupeville and salamanders in Clinton). Although these two towns share an island and are only about 27 miles away from each other, Clinton tends to be south of the rain shadow (and is often in the *convergence zone*).

However, keep in mind that even though mountains don't move, the rain shadow can shift sometimes. If the dominant winds shift to a more northerly flow, for instance, the rain shadow falls more to the south of the mountains–suddenly Seattle/Tacoma could be the dry zone. But it won't last.

Cherie and father Wayne Ude enjoy sun on Orcas Island, which receives less than 30 inches of rain a year, being part of the banana belt. In fact, water supply can be an issue on the dry and rocky island. Instead of overgrown rainforest (jungle), Orcas is reminiscent of Rocky Mountain forests with more visibility and easy walking.

A slight haze combined with a clear mountain in the background hint at an *inversion* that is trapping air in more congested areas on the mainland.

Photo by Marian Blue

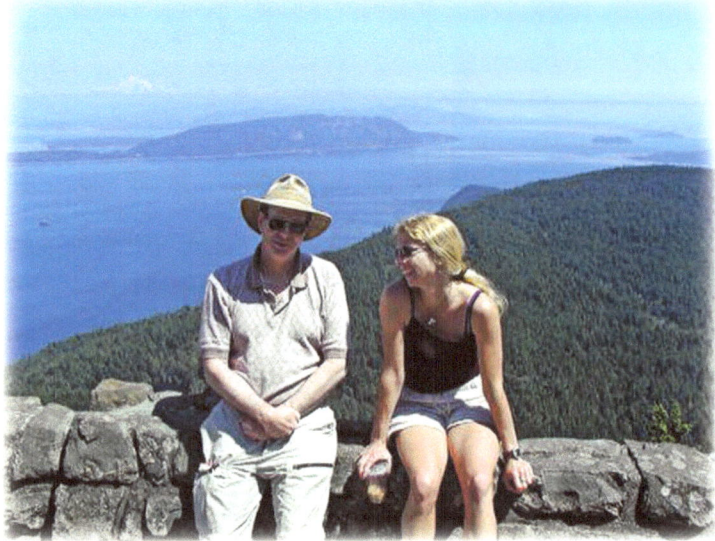

MEANWHILE, BACK IN THE RAINFOREST...

Fungi and mushrooms provide wild color and immense variety in Northwet rainforests, one of the wettest nontropical environments in the world. Some trees form symbiotic relationships with fungi because nutriments in the shallow soil are few. Other fungi help with decomposition, which also adds nutriments to the soil.

Hundreds of species provide an amazing variety of shapes and sizes. Some such as ganoderma applanatum (found in the Northwet) are bioluminescent (glow in the dark) for those who want to brave the wet dark to seek them out.

Mushroom hunters sometimes become very possessive of the sites where the best edible mushrooms are found, but a number of clubs and organizations exist to help newbies find appropriate sites and non-lethal fungi. People in these groups prowl the woods in search of the fungal wonders, especially in the first rains after a July-August dry patch or during March and April when rains taper off a little.

Some permits and/or restrictions apply to mushroom hunting. Check with the Puget Sound Mycological Society for details. For those who are willing to look and not eat, the Northwet provides almost as much fungal color on the ground as it does brilliant color in the sky.

Mushroom experts advise that you begin your mushroom adventures with a group to avoid misadventures such as poisoning, getting lost, or drowning in a deluge. Even experts don't always agree on what is edible and what is not. This yellow jelly is described as "poisonous," "inedible," and "edible" depending on which source you use. To find these possibly edible delicacies, ramp up your weather gear: high boots and breathable rain jacket with a hood are essential.

Photo by Marian Blue

Finding a lost ball in a rainforest is like looking for a dry spot in the Northwet. Finding mushrooms is much less challenging but knowing the edible from those that not-even-a-slug will eat is tough.

Photos by Marian Blue

Photos by Marian Blue

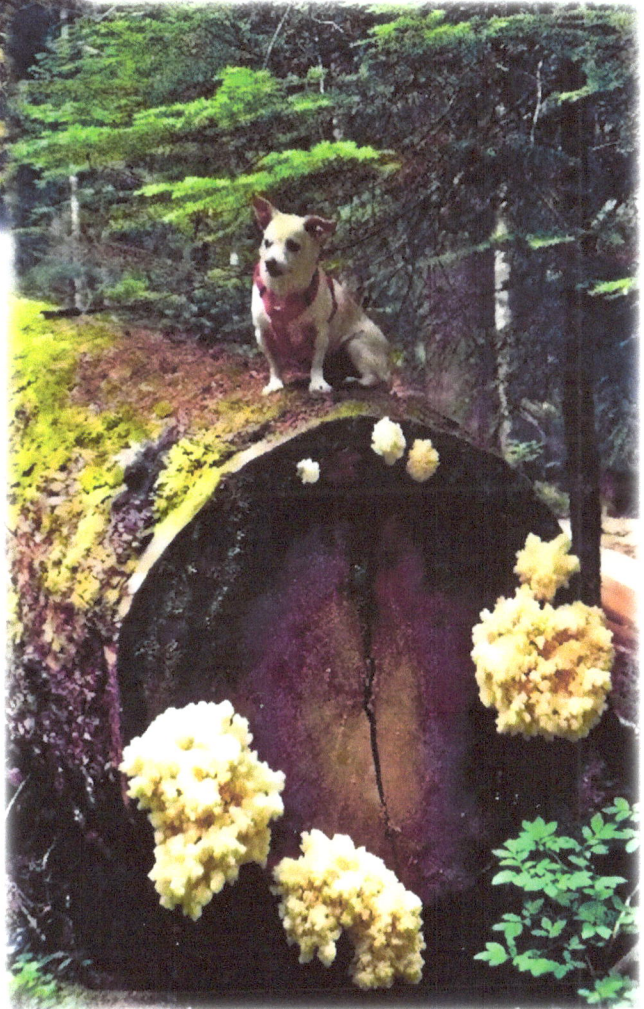

Skunk cabbage can sprout in what looks like dry ground.

In addition to fungi, many other plants are common in the Northwet Rainforests. Sometimes, as early as February, you may see yellow skunk cabbage sprouting through what appears to be dry duff. Skunk cabbage loves wet, even saturated ground. You could find yourself suddenly knee-deep in boggy mud. Besides, if you step on a skunk cabbage, you'll learn how it received its name. This clever plant emits warmth as well, melting chilly snow, for instance, around it. Skunk cabbage is a true northwet individual along with fungus, moss, and slugs.

Many mushrooms are short-lived but beautiful. Hunting them to photograph is almost a daily activity.
Photo by Marian Blue

SEASONS

People in the Northwet enjoy claiming four seasons because the terms "spring, summer, fall, and winter" are commonly used in school books and television shows; also, calendars indicate when spring, summer, fall, and winter occur, so the seasons must be real. However, people who claim four seasons in the Northwet have a 50% chance of never having been to geographical locations that go through four seasons (like Colorado) or they have a 50% chance of having become delusional, which can happen if moss begins to grow in the ears (unless you're wood folk or bigfoot).

In fact, the Northwet has one season, the Wet Season (see *Water Year* under *Year*). Sometimes, people are confused by the drier and sunnier months of July and August, which resemble, in many ways, a Colorado summer, which is hotter longer and where things dry out between brief thunderstorms. That kind of day is most noticeable by echoing cries of "I want to move here!" from tourists.

Ultimately, Northwet summer illusions tend to wash away in a long series of soggy days; it's been known to pour almost an inch of rain in one day in Seattle during August.

Although fall color pops out in higher elevations, October deciduous leaves tend to

Higher elevations give fall color enthusiasts lots of chances to experience a more genuine Fall provided they take a road trip.

Photo by Lynne Hann

Sailing is year-round activity, but warmer weather lures more sailors to take up the tiller. However, summer is also when winds are lighter, making chillier months more exhilarating with rambunctious winds.

Sailboat photo by Cherie Ude

simply turn soggy brown and plop to the ground. Many residents ride into the mountains to enjoy more typical fall colors where clear blue skies and crisp colors put cameras to work creating calendar and travel brochure fodder.

As to winter, some plants do lose their leaves during the chillier months; this may be a combination of cooler temperatures and excess water.

Winter can ignite daydreams of donning wool socks and walking hand and hand through the wonderland ... just don't forget to make your top layer foul weather attire! Such typical winter is short-lived in the Northwet lower elevations.

Photo by Lynne Hann

In that time that could be called winter, frost, ice, and even snow occur in lower elevations, but within a couple days, these tend to wash away below another *atmospheric river*. Snow quickly transforms into floods.

Spring is perhaps one of the most deceptive of the season illusions. Slight rises in temperature encourage plants to bloom brilliantly, especially the Skagit Valley daffodil and tulip fields and the abundant rhododendrons that populate the Northwet. Such abundant flowering has a 75%

The Skagit tulip fields lure people from miles away to visit and inhale the promise of spring. Normal wet and cold weather rarely dampens the spring euphoria.

Photo by Lynne Hann

chance of starting in February, which is quickly followed by chilling, brief snows and abundant rain in March. At the very least, several more inches of rain are to follow before the drier months of July and August. Yet every year when the abundant plants begin their color competition, Northwet residents feel hope bloom in their hearts and their calls rise with the voices of tree frogs: "Spring! Early spring! It's here!" Reality soon washes the ebullience away.

So each month of the *Water Year* passes with various illusions that pertain to the seasons found in other parts of the country.

Apples tend to ripen as September is washed away, and October reminds residents that their flood insurance is due. Gnats and mosquitoes appear in great numbers about the same time some plants begin to bloom. Some microclimates imitate one season while others take on another. Also, different elevations and microclimates can make seasons seem real ... valid. Yet the wise resident has foul weather gear for all seasons, maybe with a mosquito net for spring, a lighter weight and breathable for summer, higher boots for fall, and some with fleece lining and rubber boots with cleats for winter. However, at no time is the wise resident seen out and about with no rain gear at all.

Rhodies often bloom before the ground dries, before the chill leaves, and before the days begin to lighten. Perhaps that is one reason they're very popular with residents–that and the fact that they thrive in the wet climate.

Photo by Cherie Ude

Sun ... with ...

Yes, Virginia, there is a sun!

One doesn't often hear the word "sun" without also hearing modifiers or conditional clauses;

even a prediction of "sunny" tends to be "clear sun," maybe an expression of surprise. If during the times you hear "Sunny!" (most often in July and August), and you don't want to carry a raincoat (you're an incomer, right?), at least buy one of those plastic ponchos to stuff in a pocket. What you'll most likely hear, rather than "sun" is a version of what one optimistic forecaster offered to offset the predicted rainy weather due to an oncoming storm: "You may even possibly see a sunbreak."

Where is the dinghy?

Other terms related to *sun* offer a variety of not-so-sunny conditions, but the more often people hear the word *sun,* the happier they are. Therefore, a host of phrases that include the word sun (*partly sunny, sunbreaks, mostly sunny, filtered sun, etc.*) can mean a sky that is blue, gray, black, or anything between. Conditions can range from dry to wet.

FILTERED SUN

Sunlight through a cloud layer; the cloud layer is so light that you may be able to tell precisely where the sun is. Cloud shapes are probably not discernable. The overall effect is gray but, perhaps, bright enough to call for sunglasses. The air may feel dry. Don't forget the rain gear.

An eagle meditates on a filtered sun day. The time could be any o'clock from daylight to dusk, but it's obvious that light is coming from somewhere.

Photo by Cherie Ude

PARTLY SUNNY

Maybe sun … maybe not. Akin to *partly cloudy.* One recent forecast offered "Partly cloudy with a chance of showers. Rain or snow likely in the afternoon. Breezy at times." This is the half-full/half-empty glass question; whatever your answer, remember that there is water in the glass. Always. Have your rain gear nearby.

SUNBREAKS

Most people who live outside the Northwet never hear *sunbreak* in their weather forecasts. That's because most people live in areas where seeing the sun isn't cause for elation. Imagine high noon dark: you're wearing your headlamp to walk to the car to go for lunch. Suddenly a shaft of light, like those that shine down from alien saucers in movies, blasts into a nearby area. Sunbreak! Before you can decide to go to the beach, it's gone.

Residents learn to take immediate action if sunbreaks occur. Meetings end. Open recess occurs in schools. Cars stop on freeways, and drivers flop across car hoods to bathe in the miraculous light. That's a sunbreak.

Of course, you need rain gear. As previously mentioned, these vanish as suddenly as they appear.

Sunbreak!
There on that mountain!
Quick!
Take a picture ...
or maybe a plane!
Photo by Marian Blue

Sunbreaks have a lot in common with other colorful Northwet effects caused by a mix of light and moisture. This especially includes crepuscular effects.
Sunbreaks can be as startling and blinding as they are short lived.

Road sunbreak picture by Marian Blue
Sky sunbreaks by Lynne Hann

SUNNY

"Sunny" with bright yellow sun and blue sky occurs most often in either July or August (after July 1 and before Labor Day). Seattle, for instance, averages about 58 "clear" days a year, but the definition of clear is a sky that contains less than 30% cloud cover. In Seattle, 30% can be a lot of rain. Then there is the question of what, exactly, constitutes "cloud cover." (See *Rain* above for percentage information.) All 58 of those "clear" days may appear in the 8 ½ week period mentioned above, and it's possible none of them will be cloudless (or dry).

Debates also rage about how many sunny days **really** show up in the Northwet in part because of rain shadows, convergence zones, and other geographical influences that create micro-climates. If, for instance, Seattle is baking under blue skies and "clear" sun while it's raining at the airport, does that constitute a "clear" day? Debate also hinges on the definition of "sunny"; when one's standards of light acceptability are low, or even off, "filtered sun," for instance, can be blinding. One way to identify residents from visitors is to stand in a parking lot outside a large store or mall on a *sunny* day. The people who walk outdoors into the sunlight and duck, covering

The entire year offers those sunny days that fill calendars, brochures, and books, yet the exact number of those sunny days remains a mystery. Don't forget to keep your foul weather gear nearby.

Fair weather sailing photo by Lynne Hann

their heads with their arms and then slowly looking about, squinting, are residents. Once the sun is identified, sunglasses are immediately put on and the rain jacket may be taken off and just carried. A native may do a dance.

On a truly clear day when the sky appears blue and sunlight glints off water and snowcapped peaks, most people run for their cameras or begin using their phones to collect images. The calendars, magazines, TV broadcasts, and brochures all contain pictures taken during one of these days (remember that this is usually July or August); accompanying verbiage avoids discussing how many such photo ops there are, but that doesn't matter when millions of photos result from a single day.

Sun glinting off tree top snow provides the illusion of warm, maybe even dry footing. Don't forget the rubber boots!

Photo by Cherie Ude

THUNDERSTORMS

With all the rain and cloud variety, you may think you can expect many dramatic thunderstorms, but you'll be disappointed at how few appear in the Northwet. Western Washington rains are more like wet blankets: musty, damp, and grey.

The ocean is mostly to blame for the lack of drama. The temperature variations (lapse rate) are minimal, so one gets little super-saturation and rising currents of air to form those towering, anvil-shaped clouds that indicate a major lightning show in the wings. The Pacific itself is cool (swimming without a wet suit, even in July/August, is akin to sitting in a tub full of ice).

On the other hand, the ocean also helps generate impressive wind storms that are every bit as dramatic as many thunderstorms.

Interestingly, thunderstorms have become more common in recent years. That could be related to climate change. Whatever the cause, residents tend to get almost as excited by thunder as they do by sunbreaks,

Winds sculpt clouds into warnings of what is coming. The air fills with a rain of needles, limbs, leaves, hats, umbrellas, and awnings. For such a big blow, inside is the place to be.

Photo by Lynne Hann

and social media fills with pictures and recordings of Puget Sound lightning shows. For instance, a storm set new records for lightning strikes across the Northwet in May 2017 with 2500 strikes reported by the National Weather Service. That storm resulted in major local news coverage and at least 40,000,000 photos.

Weather Gear

A couple items of attire are highly recommended for proper attire in the Northwet.

The first is foul-weather gear. It's made of waterproof nylon, or other waterproof material; this covers the entire body with a jacket/pants combo. The pants resemble bib-overalls. The hooded jacket should have reflective tape, so people can see you in the gloom. Attach a whistle, so you can be found should you be washed into the unknown. This gear is large enough to pull over almost anything you choose to wear, including a bulky sweater or evening gown.

If you're feeling under-dressed for a special occasion in this gear, a hooded, long raincoat is an option (trench coat style). One that zips tightly is best; if it has only a tie, you'll be hindered by the coat flapping up into your face in the Northwet breezes. The assumption for such flimsy attire is that you are never outside for more than five steps between the vehicle door and the building door.

Next, of course, is rubber boots. Three pairs are good: low (ankle high), medium (calf length), and high (hip waders can be effective but only if you're in no danger of sinking; full waders can drag you down faster than a sunbreak can wink into a deluge). In answer to fashion needs, rubber boots come in many colors and styles, including high heels. They also come with a variety of linings.

As mentioned before, strap-on cleats are available and will help you stay more-or-less upright when water shifts from liquid to solid.

Not everyone uses rubber boots. Advocates of sandals claim year-round use is fine by wearing wool socks with them in chillier times. Supposedly wool helps feet stay warm even if the socks are soaked. If one doesn't mind constantly wet feet

Full rain gear should cover head to foot. If a wind is driving the rain, then goggles are useful. If it's a cold wind, covering cheeks and chin is a good idea; Darth Vadar masks are available. If you're experiencing sleet or freezing rain, then the entire reason you're outside must be reconsidered. Ask yourself, for instance, if you're being paid to be out there.

Photo by Georges Jansoone
Self-photographed
from Wikipedia Commons

and wet wool perfume, these are fine. For formal occasion, consider sewing sequins on the socks.

Don't forget to have a hard hat handy. Stow it with the life raft and flotation devices.

For "clear" sun days, especially in July and August, pocket rain gear can work. In the Northwet, you can find many rain jackets that wad into a fist-sized packet for your purse, pocket, or water-proof backpack. Keep in mind that rain may be in pockets or bands, so watch out for puddles and mini-micro-climates.

UMBRELLAS

Few natives or long-term residents of the Northwet bother with umbrellas. As noted previously, umbrellas fail to protect one from heavy mist, fog, and wind-driven, horizontal rain, sleet and related moisture. In addition, Northwet winds tend to invert umbrellas. Umbrellas also require at least one hand to keep them from beating you about the head. In addition, once set down in a cab, on a bus, in a store, or in a restaurant, umbrellas activate a memory-fail spell, which means owners can't remember to pick them up again. In fact, if you want an umbrella, just ask for one at lost and found where boxes of them reside. Hoods on jackets or coats are preferred; these leave your hands free to try to protect whatever you're carrying (pizza, files, small children, puppies).

RAIN STANCE

In addition to attire, developing good rain techniques will benefit you. This is often a matter of personal style combined with necessity. A couple stances cover the extremes.

1. Hunch and Run

Grasp hood by the front, pulling it down and forward as much as possible (if you buy a drawstring hood, this won't be needed). Bend neck, round shoulders, bend slightly at the waist, and sprint (if footing allows). Note that you won't be the only person doing this, so expect collisions.

2. Native Cool

Stand straight and stroll. Smile. Avoid squinting into the rain, fog, or sun. If you have pockets, put your hands in them. Sandals suit this stance. Eat lots of vitamin C. Hide a headlamp somewhere on your body.

WEATHER SYSTEMS

No one apparently knows how or when storms became systems, but this may be related to our culture becoming more high-tech. A weather system is the combination of elements that brings the pot to a boil. This boiling cauldron of wind, cold, rain, snow, sleet, etc. incite people on the street to complain about the storm. Meanwhile, forecasters explain the conditions as part of a weather system. People who are confused but cautious curse the weather storm system.

Added to the confusion is that many systems (not just hurricanes) are named these days, sometimes differently depending on which forecaster is speaking. This has become increasingly prevalent since 2010. National weather organizations such as NOAA (National Oceanic and Atmospheric Administration) and NWS (National Weather Service) have refrained from this winter weather system naming, but the tendency remains popular with the media who want to emphasize the drama of whatever you're enduring.

Because of this naming tendency, you'll hear different terms from different sources. For instance, the 2018 Winter Storm Polly on one national weather channel is probably a Winter Storm Alert from NOAA and a Weather System on the local channel.

Setting aside the general confusion, if you hear "system," assume "storm." If you hear a storm's name, assume "storm." Since you have all your rain gear handy anyway, the name doesn't matter. Rain by any other name is just as wet.

WIND

Winds arrive on the West Coast with the high energy of thousands of miles of open ocean fueling them. No mountains, buildings, or trees clutter the open Pacific. Consequently, high wind warnings are common. Gusts sometimes approach hurricane strength, and waves along the coast are sometimes 40–60 feet high. Trees fall. Power lines fall. Roads, littered with broken trees and power lines, become impassable. Interestingly, the rain is

Falling trees in the Northwet are common and take out anything in their path including power lines, autos, and roofs. Neither rain gear nor hard hats will help.

Photo from Wikipedia Commons

often light to nonexistent when wind rips through the Northwet, but don't count on that. The rain tends to follow the wind, dampening the energy of residents sitting in homes that are even darker and colder than usual. After the power has gone out, the next rumble you hear won't be thunder but rather the low rumble of long-time residents' generators. Some people find the sound comforting, like big cats purring in the woods. Whether you have a generator or not, don't go out whenever forecasters provide high wind warnings; they don't have terms to make you feel good about those. Even if falling rain isn't an issue, falling trees are. Your rain gear has limits on protection even if you utilize the hard hat.

Modern residents tend to dismiss wind as an issue when they plan their dwelling location. Members of the Quileute Tribe tended to be more sensible, moving farther inland during the winter months. They told stories about Thunderbird, a monstrous creature whose flapping wings were responsible for thunder and strong winds. Don't mess with the Thunderbird.

The Mukilteo/Clinton ferry sometimes provides riders with amusement park type rides when the wind comes charging down Possession Sound. This photo was taken during a wind storm on March 16, 2016 while the photographer was helping a friend battle the waves crashing over the bulkhead. Residents understand flooding.
Photo by Danielle Pennington

YEAR

Western Washington has its own "year" measurements that are dependent on precipitation.

Water year is based on the annual rainfall between October 1 and September 30 of the following year. This marks the beginning of the "wet season" to the end of that season (that's right – the "wet season" is 12 months long; see *Seasons* for what this does to traditional calendar concerns). The Water Year avoids the necessity of trying to re-set rain measurements in the middle of the heaviest rains on January 1, a date that has no logical beginning or ending in the Great Northwet. Rather, the end of September usually ends the driest part of the year and makes for a handy place to start the new Water Year.

Residents don't usually celebrate October 1 as the new year because they don't like to admit that their lives are ruled by water rather than calendars.

Other states also have arbitrary water years, some starting in July, for instance; logic is not the dictate but, rather, moisture. Perhaps that is a form of logic if you're wet. Few other places in the continental states have quite as definitive a break as Western Washington does during the July-August time period. However, even during that time, if you venture into a rainforest, expect damp. Actually, if you venture outside, expect damp.

Perhaps it's instinct, but this child already has learned two basic rules for survival in the Great Northwet:
1. Always seek out the light.
2. Always keep the rubber boots handy!

Photo by Racheal J. Brager

From pluviophile to sun worshipper, people have many reasons for living in the Western Northwest. Sometimes those reasons are because of the temperate, marine climate and sometimes they are in spite of that climate. Adaptation is the key

…with good weather gear.

Whatever mood the Pacific Northwest presents, underlying surf song and rainforest mist capture the imagination and lure people ever deeper into soggy embrace.

Photo by Lynne Hann

About the Author

Marian Blue has lived in climates ranging from the dramatic chill within the shadow of Mt. Sopris, Colorado to the sunny warmth of the Dominican Republic in the Caribbean. The most challenging environment for her has been within the mossy and dark shadows in the misty Northwet. Always hoping for sunny weather, she watched weather forecasts diligently and began to notice a wide variety of terms and probability terms (possible, chance of, likelihood of, and could even be ...) that always hinted at sunshine lurking somewhere within those shadows. This has led not only to this book but also to *How Many Words For Rain,* a book of poetry with photographs by Lynne Hann.

Photo by Cherie Ude

In addition to becoming a weather-obsessed individual, Marian Blue has been a writer of fiction, poetry, essays, and journalism since the 1970s. Her award-winning work has appeared in books, magazines, newspapers, and online sites. She has also edited various publications and was founding editor for *Soundings Review.* Books she has edited include *Sea of Voices, Isle of Story* (co-edited with Celeste Mergens) and *Southeast Writers Handbook.* She is also co-author of *Artie Kane: Music to My Years–Life and Love Between the Notes.*

Blue has taught writing and literature in various locations, the most recent at Skagit Valley College; she retired in December 2016. She now spends her time writing and editing in the woods of South Whidbey where she tends her small farm of chickens, ducks, guineas, turkeys and one goose along with goats, a llama and, inside, 5 dogs, 2 parrots, and a hedgehog. They all know how to swim.
For more information, her full bio appears on Amazon (author page) and on her Webpage at Sunbreak Press (www.sunbreakpress.com).

www.ingramcontent.com/pod-product-compliance
Lightning Source LLC
Chambersburg PA
CBHW061154030426
42336CB00003B/44